RUBANK EDUCATIONAL LIBRARY

SELECTED STUDIES

Advanced Etudes, Scales and Arpeggios in All Major and All Minor Keys

by H. Voxman

ADVANCED ETUDES

SCALES AND ARPEGGIOS

SPECIAL STUDIES

RUBANK®

HAL•LEONARD® CORPORATION
7777 W. BLUEMOUND RD. P.O. BOX 13819 MILWAUKEE, WI 53213

Bb Major

BALASANIAN

Copyright MCMLII by Rubank, Inc., Chicago, Ill.
International Copyright Secured

G Minor

BLAZHEVICH

Eb Major

VOBARON

Allegretto (in one)

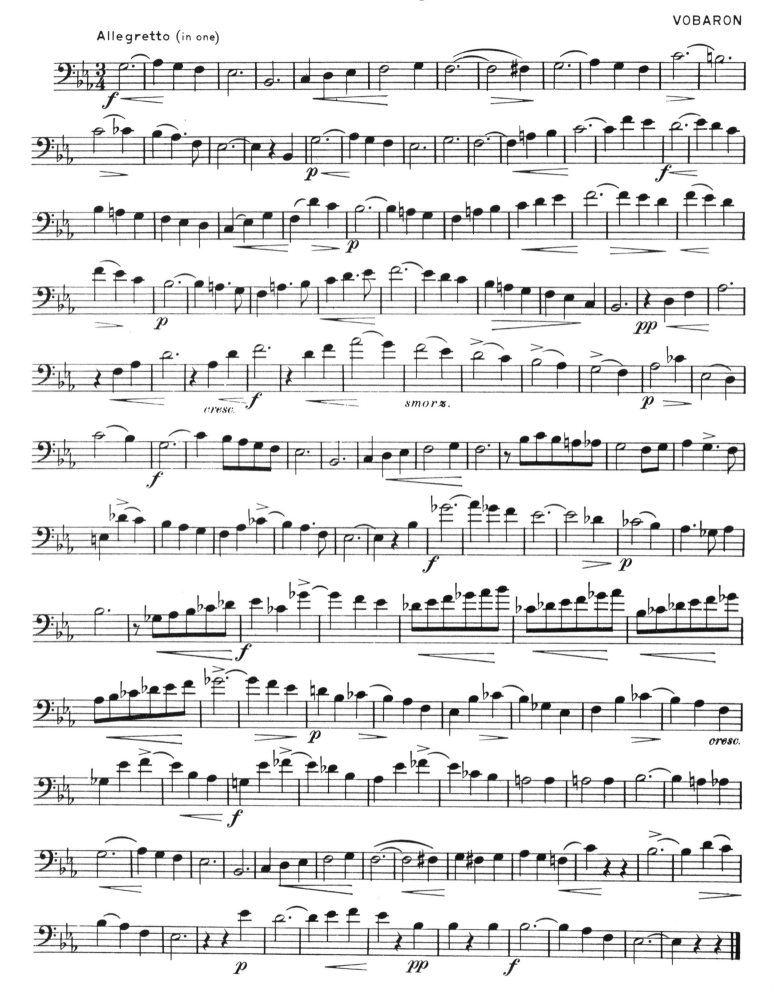

BELCKE

C Minor

BLAZHEVICH

BÖHME

F Major

MÜLLER

Allegretto

MÜLLER

Allegro moderato

D Minor

GATTI

BÖHME

Valse lentement

Ab Major

GATTI

BÖHME

F Minor

BLAZHEVICH

Allegretto

Allegretto affettuoso

C Major

VOBARON

GATTI

A Minor

ROSSARI

Db Major

BLAZHEVICH

BLAZHEVICH

Allegro moderato

f energico

B♭ Minor

CORNETTE

BÖHME

Allegretto

G Major

BLAZHEVICH

Andante con moto

As fast as technic permits

E Minor

GATTI

KOPPRASCH

Allegro vivace (moderate two)

G♭ Major

DUHEM

Adagio cantabile

BÖHME

Allegro ma non troppo

Eb Minor

BLAZHEVICH

GATTI

Allegro mosso

D Major

BLAZHEVICH

BLAZHEVICH

Veloce

poco accellerando e molto cresc.

B Minor

Moderato

BLAZHEVICH

C♭ Major

JOHANSON

Allegro

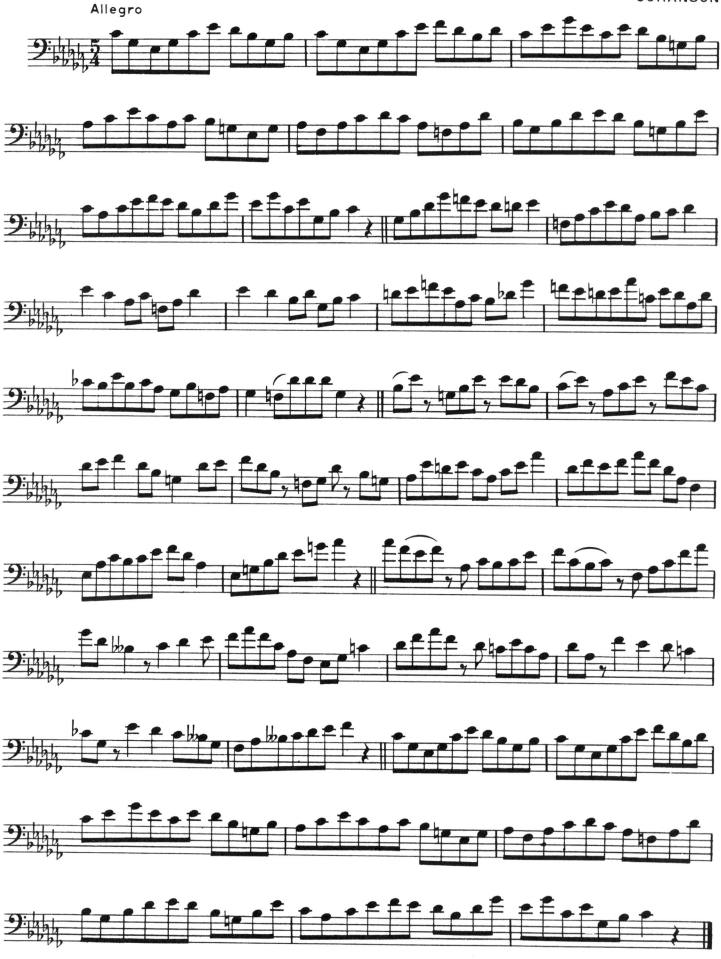

ROSSARI

Allegretto

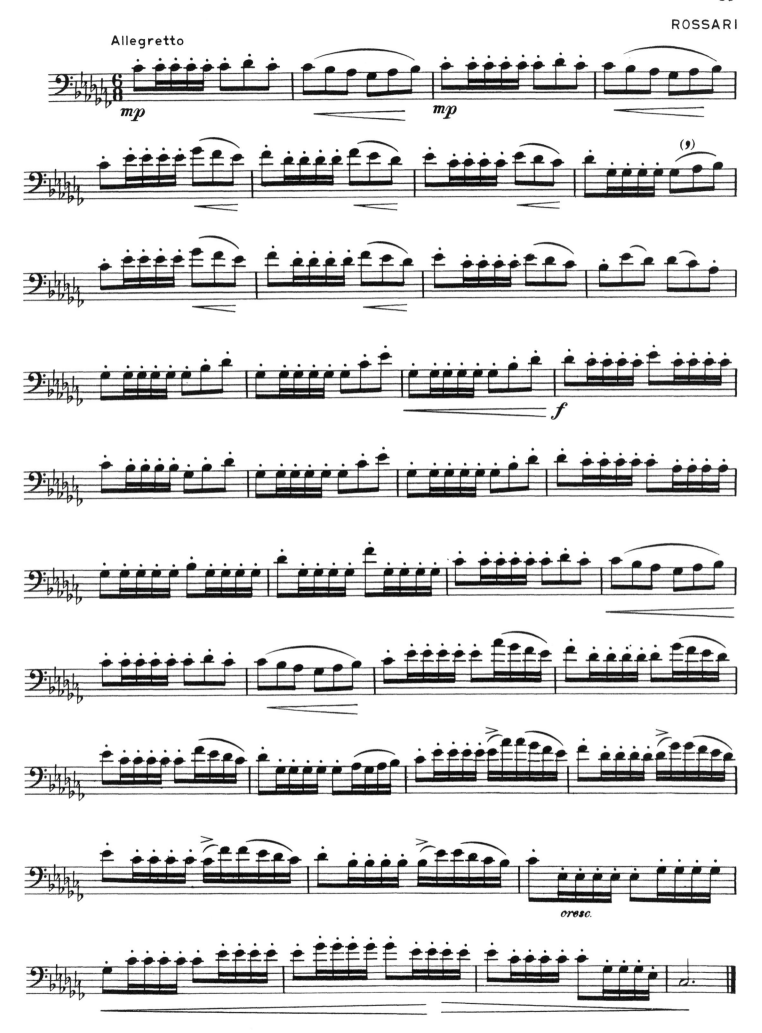

A♭ Minor

BLAZHEVICH

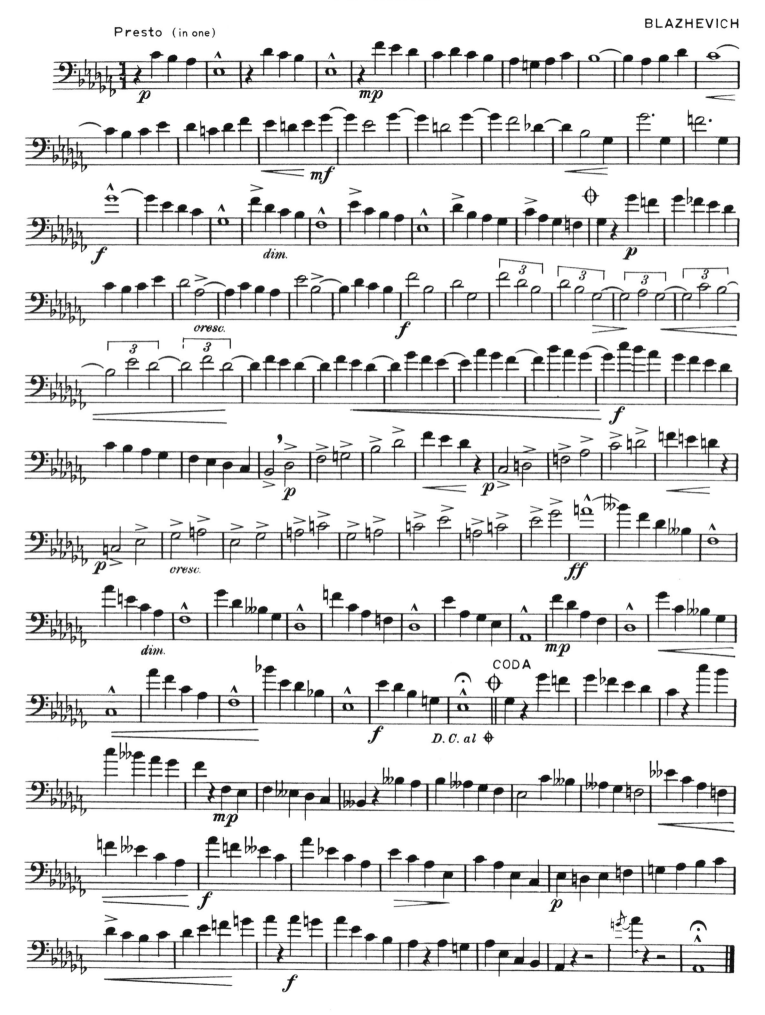

SCHERZO

BAGANTZ

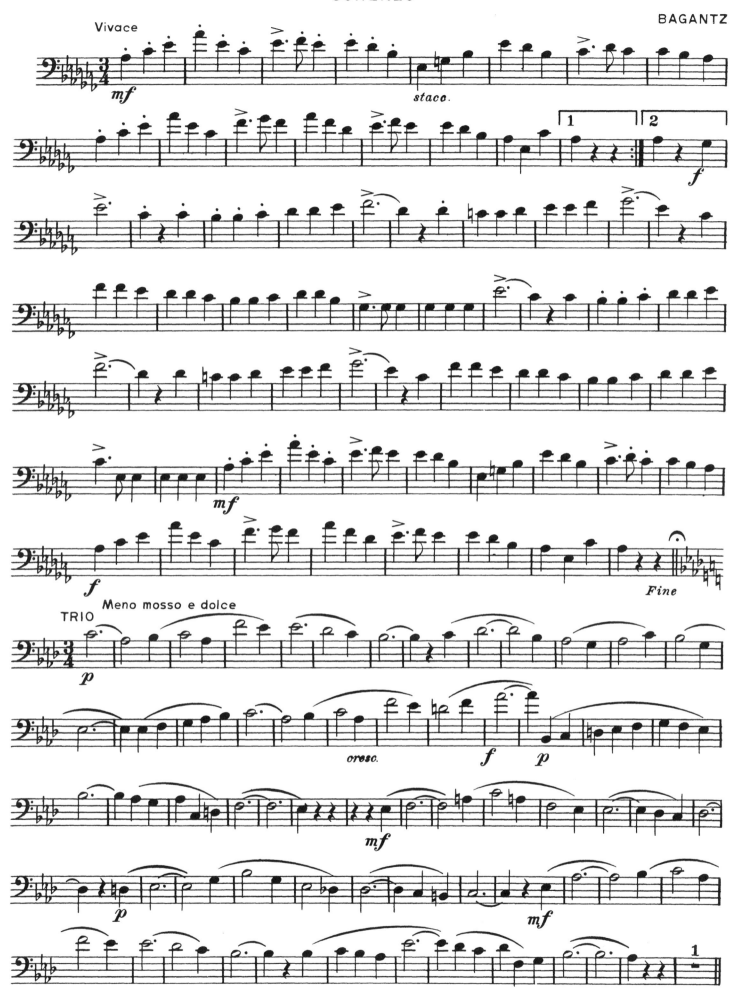

Scherzo D.C. al Fine

A Major

BELCKE

Allegro vivace

Andante affettuoso

DIEPPO

F# Minor

VOBARON

ROSSARI

Allegro moderato

E Major

DIEPPO

BLAZHEVICH

C# Minor

BLAZHEVICH

BLAZHEVICH

B Major

ROSSARI

Adagio

JOHANSON

G♯ Minor

ROSSARI

Allegretto comodo

BLAZHEVICH

Velocity

St. JACOME
(adapted)

Scales

The use of a metronome with the following studies is highly recommended.

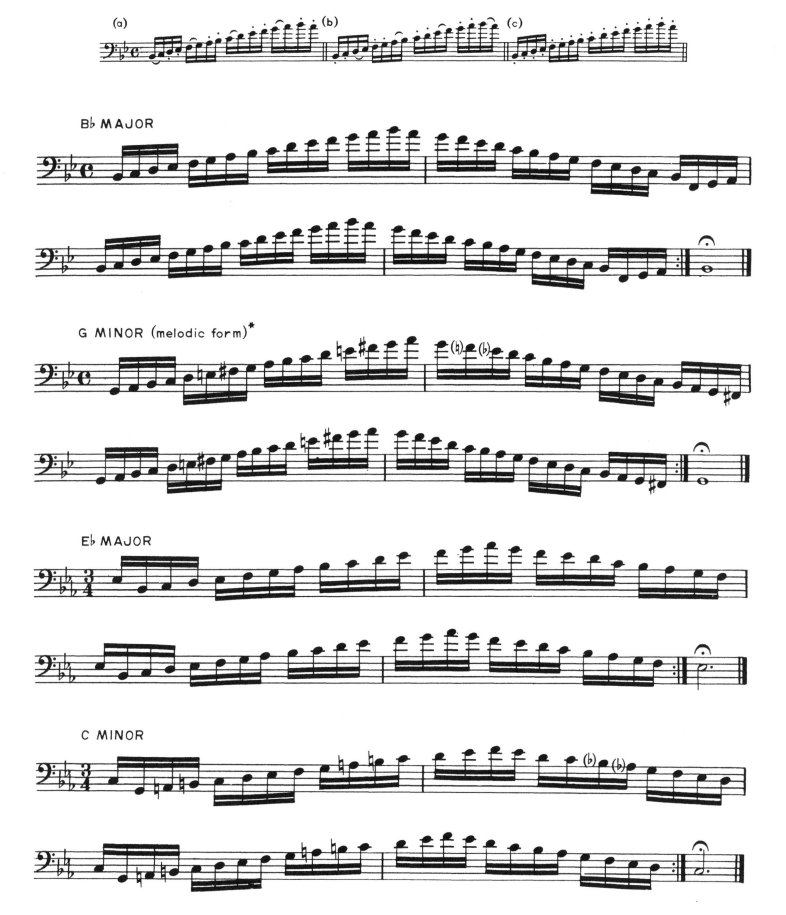

Bb MAJOR

G MINOR (melodic form)*

Eb MAJOR

C MINOR

* All minor scale exercises should also be practiced in the harmonic form.

56

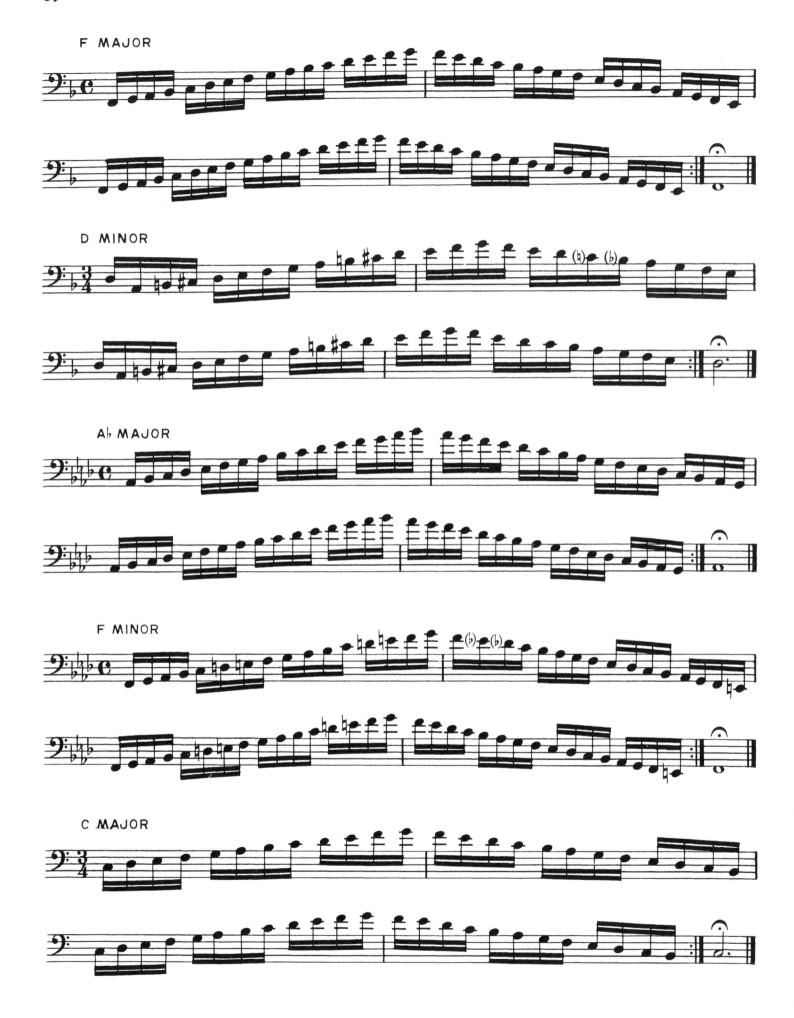

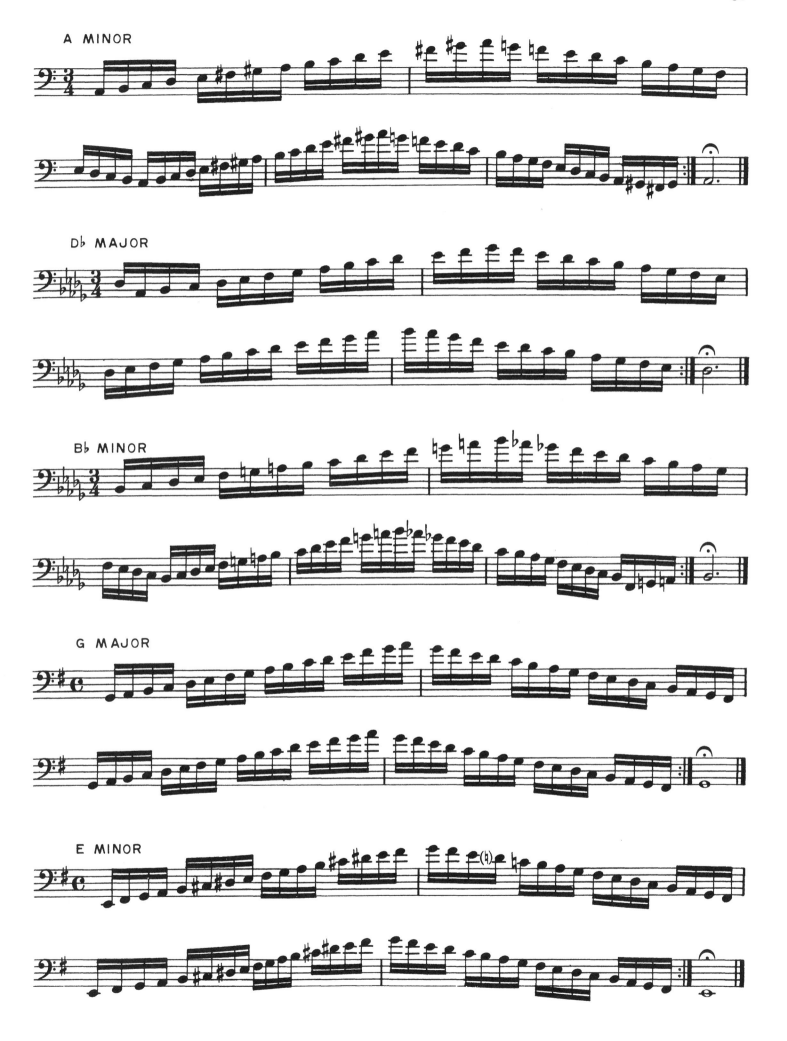

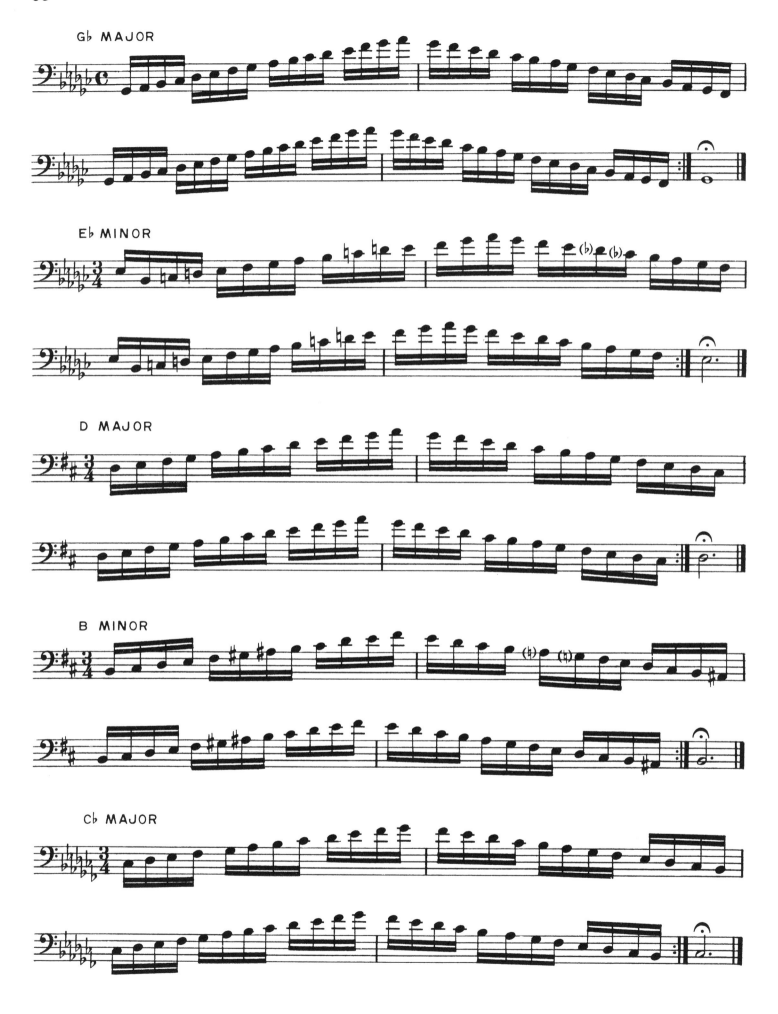

B MAJOR

G# MINOR

Whole tone scale on E

Whole tone scale on F

Chromatic Scale

Chromatic Study

Practice with various articulations

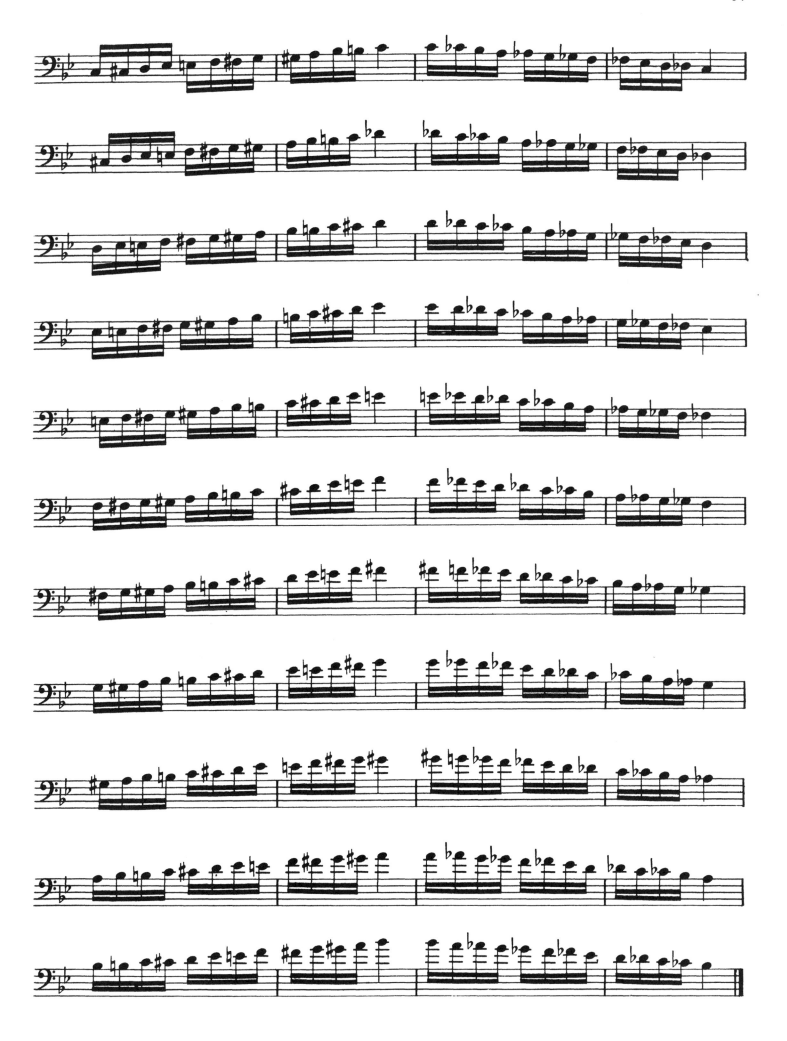

62

Arpeggios

64

Cb MAJOR

Ab MINOR

A MAJOR

F# MINOR

E MAJOR

C# MINOR

B MAJOR

G# MINOR

Arpeggio of the augmented 5th

Interval Studies

BAGANTZ

ARBAN

Apply to Nos. 3 Through 10:

ARBAN

CORNETTE

Clef Studies

BELCKE-MÜLLER

Adagio espressivo

Tempo alla polacca

BALASANIAN

Cadenza Studies